Written by Evelyn Coleman

Celebration Press
An Imprint of Addison-Wesley
Educational Publishers, Inc.

What if I had some sticks?

What if I had some stones?

What if I had some paint?

What if I had some brushes?

What if I had some string?

What if I had some feathers?

I would have some birds.